the heart of
a volunteer

Compiled by Dan Zadra
Designed by Steve Potter and Jenica Wilkie

COMPENDIUM™
PUBLISHING

live inspired.

ACKNOWLEDGEMENTS

These quotations were gathered lovingly but unscientifically over several years and/or contributed by many friends or acquaintances. Some arrived—and survived in our files—on scraps of paper and may therefore be imperfectly worded or attributed. To the authors, contributors and original sources, our thanks, and where appropriate, our apologies.
—The Editors

WITH SPECIAL THANKS TO

Jason Aldrich, Gerry Baird, Jay Baird, Neil Beaton, Josie Bissett, Jan Catey, Doug Cruickshank, Jim Darragh, Jennifer & Matt Ellison, Rob Estes, Michael Flynn & Family, Shannan Frisbie, Jennifer Hurwitz, Heidi Jones, Cristal & Brad Olberg, Janet Potter & Family, Diane Roger, Jenica Wilkie, Clarie Yam & Erik Lee, Kobi, Heidi & Shale Yamada, Justi, Tote & Caden Yamada, Robert & Val Yamada, Kaz, Kristin, Kyle & Kendyl Yamada, Tai & Joy Yamada, Anne Zadra, August & Arline Zadra.

CREDITS

Compiled by Dan Zadra
Designed by Kobi Yamada and Steve Potter

We rise by lifting others.

-ROBERT GREEN INGERSOLL

The Power of One

The little things? The little moments? They aren't little.

—STEVEN POTTER

There isn't a problem in this world that can't be solved. The hard part is convincing people that we are all part of the solution— that each of us has something to give which cannot otherwise be given.

The "power of one"—that's something we have all heard. It's not just a theory, or a slogan or a philosophy, it's more like a mathematical miracle. I like to call it the arithmetic of the heart, and you will hear it echoed over and over in the pages of this book. It sounds like this:

When it comes to helping others, there are no little things…the accumulation of a lot of little things isn't little…it takes each of us to make a difference for all of us…none of us can do everything at once, but all of us can do something at once…one person can make a difference, and every person must try…just concentrate on helping one person, giving hope to one person, and that person in turn may give hope to somebody else and it will spread out.

Using the arithmetic of the heart, one person could change the social landscape of our country in a few hours a week. "If every American donated five hours a week," writes Whoopi Goldberg, "it would equal the labor of twenty million full-time volunteers."

Is five hours a week too much? Pete Santiago reminds us that if every employee in every American company were given just four hours a month to volunteer for a cause of their choice, American companies could transform thousands of neighborhoods and millions of lives.

It's the greatest mistake to do nothing because you can only do a little. Give what you can, and do it together. That's the power of one. Alone we can do so little; together we can do so much.

Dan Zadra

A   V   O   L   U   N   T   E   E   R

It's time for some heart work.

—RAINER MARIA RILKE

There are unrecognized heroes among our ordinary neighbors.

—HAROLD W. BERNARD

Every day thousands of unsung heroes bring caring and compassion to the lives of millions. Their names are never featured in the headlines, but our world would be a much darker place without them.

—CHARLES DEVLIN

The world knows nothing of its greatest people.

—HENRY TAYLOR

The greatest object in the universe, says the philoso-
pher, is a good person struggling with adversity;
yet there is a greater, which is the good person
who comes to relieve it.

—OLIVER GOLDSMITH

There are those whose lives affect all others around
them. Quietly touching one heart, who in turn,
touches another. Reaching out to ends further
than they would ever know.

—WILLIAM BRADFIELD

The people who make a difference are not the ones
with the credentials, but the ones with the concern.

—MAX LUCADO

T   H   E   H   E   A   R   T   O   F

Goodness is unobtrusive. It does not flash, it glows.

—DON WARD

I've seen and met angels wearing the disguise
of ordinary people living ordinary lives.

—TRACY CHAPMAN

There is a light in this world, a healing spirit more
powerful than any darkness we may encounter. We
sometimes lose sight of this force when there is so
much suffering and pain. Then suddenly, the spirit will
emerge through the lives of ordinary people who hear
a call and answer in extraordinary ways.

—MOTHER TERESA

A   V   O   L   U   N   T   E   E   R

Each of us can look back upon someone who made a great difference in our lives, often a teacher or a volunteer whose wisdom or simple acts of caring made an impression. In all likelihood, it was someone who sought no recognition, but the impact of their character and kindness on our lives was heroic.

—STEPHEN M. WOLF

True heroism is remarkably sober, very undramatic. It is not the urge to surpass all others at whatever cost, but the urge to serve others at whatever cost.

—ARTHUR ASHE

Everyone has the power for greatness, not for fame but greatness, because greatness is determined by service. You don't have to have a college degree to serve.

—MARTIN LUTHER KING, JR.

T H E   H E A R T   O F

They who scatter joy.
—RALPH WALDO EMERSON

All of you reading these words have loved someone, have done someone a kindness, have healed a wound, have taken on a challenge, have created something beautiful, and have enjoyed breathing the air of existence. Every moment you make a difference.
—RANDOM ACTS OF KINDNESS

The capacity to do the right thing, to dare to take a stand and make a difference, is within you now. The question is: When the moment arrives, will you remember you're a hero and selflessly respond in support of those in need?
—ANTHONY ROBBINS

A V O L U N T E E R

We are the ones we've been waiting for.

—SLOGAN, SOUTHWEST SENIOR CITIZEN VOLUNTEERS

People are homeless, hungry and sick.
Somebody should do something about this.
Be somebody.

—BONNIE BRADY

Past the seeker as he prayed came the crippled
and the beggar and the beaten. And seeing them,
he cried, "Great God, how is it that a loving creator
can see such things and yet do nothing about them?"
God said, "I did do something. I made you."

—SUFI TEACHING

Volunteers are the only human beings on the face
of the earth who reflect this nation's compassion,
unselfish caring, patience, and just plain loving
one another.

—ERMA BOMBECK

May God bless you with the foolishness to think that you can make a difference in the world, so that you will do the things which others tell you cannot be done.

—OPENING PRAYER, MOTHER'S MARCH FOR CANCER

Volunteering is an act of heroism on a grand scale. And it matters profoundly. It does more than help people beat the odds; it changes the odds.

— BILL CLINTON

What volunteers bring is the human touch, the individual, caring approach that no government program, however well-meaning and well-executed can deliver.

—EDWARD JAMES OLMOS

T H E   H E A R T   O F

Volunteerism is the voice of the people put into action. These actions shape and mold the present into a future of which we can all be proud.

—HELEN DYER

This country is generous, giving, compassionate and sacrificing. Many millions contribute to United Way, drive ambulances, fight fires, save lives, help the handicapped, contribute to medical research, serve in the armed forces, encourage youth, dance with the elderly and comfort the sick.

—HARRY GRAY

Some people give time, some money, some their skills and connections, some literally give their life's blood… but everyone has something to give.

—BARBARA BUSH

A VOLUNTEER

Here's to our nation's volunteers:
All work and no pay.

—CAT LANE

The broadest, and maybe the most meaningful definition
of volunteering: "Doing more than you have to because
you want to, in a cause you consider good."

—IVAN SCHEIER

Show me a person whose car is garaged with
the grille facing out, and I'll show you a volunteer.

—UNKNOWN

T H E   H E A R T   O F

Leave your comfort zone. Go stretch yourself
for a good cause.

—KOBI YAMADA

It really is much easier to help people and causes
than what most people think. You just go out and
take that first step and things start falling into place.
You might have to change direction, but you never
pull over and park!

—JASON CROWE, FOUNDER (AT AGE 11) OF *CELLO CRIES ONE*

Even if it's a little thing, do something for those who
have a need of help, something for which you get no
pay but the privilege of doing it.

—ALBERT SCHWEITZER

A   V   O   L   U   N   T   E   E   R

I am a recipient of unconditional love, I am a volunteer.

—SHANTERRA MCBRIDE

When you volunteer, you are not paid in money or recognition, you are paid in love. People may forget what you said, and people may forget what you did, but they will never forget how you made them feel.

—UNKNOWN

You mean the world to someone. Someone you don't even know loves you for who you are and what you have done for them. Every night, someone thinks about you before they go to sleep. If not for you, someone may not be living. To the world you may be just one person, but to one person you may be the world.

—UNKNOWN

The country clubs, the cars, the boats,
your assets may be ample,
But the best inheritance you can leave
your kids is to be a good example.

—UNKNOWN

Mom was a woman who cared about the people next
door or around the world, and she did something about
it. What our mother did—not said—showed us what
caring is all about.

—FATHER ANDREW SIMMS

Live your life so that your children can tell their children
that you not only stood for something wonderful—
you acted on it.

—DAN ZADRA

A   V   O   L   U   N   T   E   E   R

There is more to life than having everything.

—MAURICE SENDAK

A wise woman who was traveling in the mountains found a precious stone in a stream. The next day she met another traveler who was hungry, and the wise woman opened her bag to share her food. The hungry traveler saw the precious stone and asked the woman to give it to him. She did so without hesitation. The traveler left, rejoicing in his good fortune. He knew the stone was worth enough to give him security for a lifetime. But a few days later he came back to return the stone to the wise woman.

"I've been thinking," he said, "I know how valuable the stone is, but I give it back in the hope that you can give me something that is far more precious. Give me what you have within you that enabled you to give me the stone."

—UNKNOWN

Time has a wonderful way of showing us what really matters.

—MARGARET PETERS

First there's the job—where the goal is simply to earn a living and support your family. Then there's the career where you trace your progress through various appointments and achievements. Finally, there's the calling—the ideal blend of activity and character that makes work inseparable from life.

—ROBERT BELLA

Throughout your life, there is a voice only you can hear. A voice which mythologists label "the call." A call to the true value of your life. If you never hear it, perhaps nothing is lost. If you hear it and ignore it, your life is lost.

—JENNIFER JAMES

T H E   H E A R T   O F

A life without cause is a life without effect.

Believe in something bigger than yourself.
Your life is worth a noble motive.

It is not enough to merely exist. It's not enough to say,
"I'm earning enough to live and support my family. I do
my work well, I'm a good parent." That's all very well,
but you must do something more, something for your
fellow man…For, remember, you don't live in a world
all your own. Your brothers are here, too.

A   V O L U N T E E R

A very important part of the joy of living
is the joy of giving.

—WILLIAM BUCK

Dedicate your life to a cause greater than yourself,
and your life will become a glorious romance
and adventure.

—MACK DOUGLAS

You've touched people and known it. You've touched
people and never may know it. Either way, no matter
what your life feels like to you right now, you have
something to give. It is in giving to one another that
each one of our lives becomes meaningful.

—LAURA SCHLESSINGER

T   H   E   H   E   A   R   T   O   F

Life's most persistent and urgent question is:
What are you doing for others?

—MARTIN LUTHER KING, JR.

We choose only once. We choose either to be warriors
or to be ordinary. A second choice does not exist.
Not on this earth.

—CARLOS CASTANEDA

When we're in our nineties and we're looking back,
it's not going to be how much money we made or
how many awards we've won. It's really, "What did
we stand for? Did we make a positive difference
for people?"

—ELIZABETH DOLE

A   V O L U N T E E R

The greatest tragedy is indifference.

—THE RED CROSS

Too many people do not care what happens as long as it does not happen to them.

—WILLIAM HOWARD TAFT

Indifference is the strongest force in the universe. It makes everything it touches meaningless. Love and hate don't stand a chance against it.

—JOAN VINGE

Bad things don't happen because you care, they happen when you don't care.

—ELIZABETH MATTHEWS

Sometimes our light goes out but is blown into flame by another human being. Each of us owes deepest thanks to those who have rekindled this light.

—ALBERT SCHWEITZER

There are spaces between our fingers so that another person's fingers can fill them in.

—UNKNOWN

As we move around this world and as we act with kindness, perhaps, or with indifference or with hostility toward the people we meet, we are setting the great spider web a-tremble. The life that I touch for good or ill will touch another life, and that in turn another, until who knows where the trembling stops or in what far place my touch will be felt.

—FREDERICK BUECHNER

T   H   E   H   E   A   R   T   O   F

Sympathy sees and says, "I'm sorry."
Compassion sees and says, "I'll help."

—UNKNOWN

We cannot live only for ourselves. A thousand fibers connect us with our fellow man; and along these fibers, as sympathetic threads, our actions run as causes, and they come back as effects.

—HERMAN MELVILLE

Lend me your hope for awhile. A time will come when I will heal, and I will lend my renewed hope to others.

—ELOISE COLE

A   V   O   L   U   N   T   E   E   R

The little things? The little moments?
They aren't little.

—STEVEN POTTER

Dr. Jo Blessing tells of an elderly patient who decided
not to commit suicide because a stranger stopped,
smiled and fed the pigeons with her in the park.
Today, without realizing it, you may be the answer
to someone's prayers.

—DAN ZADRA

Listen to a heart that is crying…because you can't
see the tears.

—MABELLE PITTMAN

T   H   E   H   E   A   R   T   O   F

If we could hear one another's prayers,
it would relieve God of a great burden.

—MICHAEL NOLAN

Unless we can hear each other singing and crying,
unless we can comfort each other's failures and cheer
each other's victories, we are missing out on the best
that life has to offer. The only real action takes place
on the bridge between people.

—UNKNOWN

Whatever there is of God and goodness in the universe,
it must work itself out and express itself through us.
We cannot stand aside and let God do it.

—ALBERT EINSTEIN

A   V O L U N T E E R

The heart that gives— gathers.

—HANNAH MOORE

The miracle is this—the more we share,
the more we have.

—LEONARD NIMOY

There is a wonderful mythical law of nature that
the three things we crave most in life—happiness,
freedom and peace of mind—are always attained
by giving them to someone else.

—KEYNOTE

If you have food in your refrigerator, clothes on your
back, and a roof over your head…you are richer than
75% of this world. If you have money in the bank and
spare change in a dish someplace…you are among the
top 8% of the world's wealthy. You are blessed in that
you have room to give to others; and if you do, the best
part is that it will come back to you ten times over.

—MICHAEL DONOHOUGH

You can give without loving, but you cannot love without giving.

—AMY CARMICHAEL

Love is a force. It is not a result; it is a cause. It is not a product; it produces. It is a power—a power for good—but it is valueless unless it's released.

—DIANE MORRISSEY

A bell's not a bell 'til you ring it.
A song's not a song 'til you sing it.
Love in your heart wasn't put there to stay.
Love isn't love 'til you give it away.

—OSCAR HAMMERSTEIN

T H E   H E A R T   O F

When you give away a little piece of your heart,
you're giving away the only thing you can give away,
which, after you do, you got more left than you had
before you gave some of it away.

—DON HUTSON

That's what I consider true generosity.
You give your all, and yet you always feel as if
it costs you nothing.

—SIMONE DE BEAUVOIR

If you help others, you will be helped. Perhaps
tomorrow, perhaps in a hundred years, but you
will be helped. Nature must pay off the debt.
It is not only a mathematical law, it is divine.

—GEORGE POSPICHEK

A   V   O   L   U   N   T   E   E   R

We rise by lifting others.
—ROBERT GREEN INGERSOLL

Do the kinds of things that come from the heart. When you do, you won't be dissatisfied, you won't be envious, you won't be longing for somebody else's things. On the contrary, you'll be overwhelmed with what comes back.
—MORRIE SCHWARTZ

If you don't like what you're getting back in life, take a look at what you're putting out.
—PAMELA DREYER

T   H   E   H   E   A   R   T   O   F

You are one of the forces of nature.
—JULES MICHELET

Unselfish acts are the real miracles out of which
all the reported miracles grow.
—RALPH WALDO EMERSON

Dare to believe in miracles. Look beyond the mud
on the windshield, beyond the impossible, and
know life is more than anguish and stress. Reach
out to someone. When your heart is too heavy to
feel sunlight or taste the rain. Rid yourself of dark
thought and melancholy. Open your mind to fresh
air, to the unlimited music in your soul.
—JOYCE SEQUICHIE HIFLER

A   V   O   L   U   N   T   E   E   R

Do not wait for leaders; do it alone, person to person.

—MOTHER TERESA

We're all trying to make a big difference, not realizing the small difference we make for each other every day.

—DAPHNE ROSE KINGMA

I have never been especially impressed by the heroics of people convinced that they are about to change the world. I am more awed by those who struggle to make one small difference after another.

—ELLEN GOODMAN

We can all be angels to one another. We can choose to obey the still small stirring voice within, the little whisper that says, "Go. Ask. Reach out. Be an answer to someone's plea."

—JOAN WESTER ANDERSON

Our world is saved one or two people at a time.

—ANDRE GIDE

There was once an elderly, despondent woman in a nursing home. She wouldn't speak to anyone or request anything. She merely existed—rocking in her creaky old rocking chair. The old woman didn't have many visitors. But every couple mornings, a concerned young nurse would go into her room. She didn't try to speak or ask questions. She simply pulled up another rocking chair beside the old woman and rocked with her. Weeks later, the old woman finally spoke. "Thank you," she said, "for rocking with me."

—UNKNOWN

The effect of one good-hearted person is incalculable.

—OSCAR ARIAS

The million little things that drop into your hands
The small opportunities each day brings
He leaves us free to use or abuse
And goes unchanging along His silent way.

—HELEN KELLER

All our acts have sacramental possibilities.

—FREYA STARK

A   V   O   L   U   N   T   E   E   R

We must exchange the philosophy of excuses—what I see or am is beyond my control—for the philosophy of responsibility.

—BARBARA JORDAN

One great, strong, unselfish soul in every community could actually redeem the world.

—ELBERT HUBBARD

What I do, you cannot do; but what you do, I cannot do. The needs are great, and none of us, including me, ever do great things. But we can do small things, with great love, and together we can do something wonderful.

—MOTHER TERESA

T   H   E   H   E   A   R   T   O   F

One song can spark a moment,
one flower can wake the dream.
One tree can start a forest,
one bird can herald spring.
One vote can change a nation,
one sunbeam lights a room.
One candle wipes out darkness,
one laugh will conquer gloom.
One step must start each journey,
one word must start a prayer.
One hope will raise our spirits,
one touch can show you care.
One voice can speak with wisdom,
one heart can know what's true.
One life can make a difference,
that difference starts with you.

—UNKNOWN

A   V O L U N T E E R

The place you are in needs you today.

—CATHERINE LOGAN

I believe that one of the most important things
to learn in life is that you can make a difference in
your community no matter who you are or where
you live.

—ROSALYNN CARTER

When the world seems large and complex,
we need to remember that great world ideals
all begin in some home neighborhood.

—KONRAD ADENAUER

From where we are, and who we are in our everyday
life, that's where we make change.

—TOSHI REAGON

It is in the shelter of each other that the people live.
—IRISH PROVERB

We are a nation of neighborhoods and communities—a brilliant diversity spread like stars, like a thousand points of light in a broad and peaceful sky.
—GEORGE H.W. BUSH

When the term "community" is used, the notion that typically comes to mind is a place in which people know and care for one another—the kind of place in which people do not merely ask, "How are you?" as a formality, but care about the answer.
—AMITAI ETZIONI

T   H   E   H   E   A   R   T   O   F

We are all longing to go home to some place we have never been—a place half-remembered and half-envisioned we can only catch glimpses of from time to time: Community. Somewhere, there are people to whom we can speak with passion without having the words catch in our throats. Somewhere a circle of hands will open to receive us, eyes will light up as we enter, and voices will celebrate with us whenever we come into our own power. Community means strength that joins our strength to do the work that needs to be done. Arms to hold us when we falter. A circle of healing. A circle of friends. Someplace where we can be free.

—STARHAWK

A   V   O   L   U   N   T   E   E   R

Where we come from in America no longer signifies anything—it's where we go, and what we do when we get there, that tells us who we are and how we contribute.

—ANNA QUINDLEN

Every gathering across the nation—whether a few on the porch of a crossroads store or massed thousands in a great stadium—is the possessor of a potentially immeasurable influence on the future.

—DWIGHT D. EISENHOWER

In every community, there is work to be done.
In every nation, there are wounds to heal.
In every heart, there is the power to do it.

—MARIANNE WILLIAMSON

T   H   E   H   E   A   R   T   O   F

The great lesson is that the sacred is in the ordinary, that it is to be found in one's daily life, in one's neighbors, friends, and family, in one's backyard.

—ABRAHAM MASLOW

If love is truly a verb, if help is a verb, if forgiveness is a verb, if kindness is a verb, then you can do something about it.

—BETTY EADIE

I used to pray that God would do this or that— but now I pray that He will guide me to do whatever I can do. I used to pray for answers, but now I'm praying for strength. I used to believe that prayer changes things, but now I know that prayer changes us—and we change things.

—MOTHER TERESA

A   V   O   L   U   N   T   E   E   R

It takes courage
for people to
listen to their
own goodness
and act on it.

—PABLO CASALS

Many are called but few get up.
—OLIVER HERFORD

The truth of the matter is that you always know
the right thing to do. The hard part is doing it.
—NORMAN SCHWARZKOPF

Each morning he'd stack up the letters he'd write—
tomorrow. And think of the friends he'd fill with
delight—tomorrow. It was too bad, indeed, he was
busy today, and hadn't a minute to stop on his way.
"More time I'll give to others," he'd say. Tomorrow.
—UNKNOWN

Don't agonize. Organize.
—FLORENCE KENNEDY

Volunteers don't necessarily have the time,
but they have the heart, so they make time.
—UNKNOWN

If every American donated just five hours a week,
it would equal the labor of twenty million full-time
volunteers.

—WHOOPI GOLDBERG

T   H   E   H   E   A   R   T   O   F

Each of us has a spark of life inside us, and we must set off that spark in one another.

—KENNY AUSUBEL

I don't care what problems we have in this country—they can be solved by people coming together and organizing.

—DOLORES HUERTA

It is astonishing how short a time it takes for very wonderful things to happen.

—FRANCES H. BURNETT

A   V   O   L   U   N   T   E   E   R

Love is the light. Forward is the motion.
—UNKNOWN

The mind gives us thousands of ways to say no,
but there's only one way to say yes, and that's
from the heart.

—SUZE ORMAN

You don't need endless time and perfect conditions.
Do it now. Do it today. Do it for twenty minutes and
watch your heart start beating.

—BARBARA SHER

T   H   E   H   E   A   R   T   O   F

Give the best that you have to the highest you know—and do it now.

—RALPH W. SOCKMAN

Do not wait for life. Be aware, at every moment, that the miracle is in the here and now.

—MARCEL PROUST

The world is full of people who are guided by good intentions; what we need is more follow-through. Instead of "we almost," let the world say about us, "we did."

—"PULPIT HELPS" MAGAZINE

A   V   O   L   U   N   T   E   E   R

A company that makes nothing but money is a poor company.

—HENRY FORD

Great companies are the ones that choose to make a difference in their communities.

—FRANKLIN OJALA

Companies with a Vision and a heart do more than just create jobs and a product. They give to those who have not; they go outside the normal business channels and deliver hope.

—LENSCRAFTERS

Success is sweetest when it's shared.

—HOWARD SCHULTZ, CEO, STARBUCKS

Being a good human being is good business.

—PAUL HAWKEN

Learn, earn, return—these are the three phases
of life.

—JACK BALOUSEK

I had a dream that every U.S. company, large and small,
spontaneously decided to give every employee four
hours of paid leave each month to volunteer for a cause
of their choice. When I awoke, I couldn't shake the
dream, and it's still with me. In four hours a month,
American companies could transform thousands of
neighborhoods and millions of lives.

—PETE SANTIAGO

T   H   E   H   E   A   R   T   O   F

Goodness is the only investment that never fails.

—HENRY DAVID THOREAU

The magnitude of our social problems will require that all citizens and companies make a commitment to volunteering as a way of life.

—GEORGE ROMNEY, FORMER MICHIGAN GOVERNOR

I personally don't know how anybody can survive running a successful business in our times without caring. The twin ideals of love and care touch everything we do. My passionate belief is that business can be fun, it can be conducted with love and be a powerful force for good.

—ANITA RODDICK, THE BODY SHOP

A   V   O   L   U   N   T   E   E   R

Forever remember that the business of life
is not merely about business, but about life.

—B.C. FORBES

When people go to work, they shouldn't have
to leave their hearts at home.

—BETTY BENDER

As long as we operate within this old paradigm,
we are separated from our heart and values
during the workday and think we will have
them back when we get home. We're all
interconnected. There is a spiritual dimension
to business just as to individuals.

—BEN (COHEN) AND JERRY (GREENFIELD)

Greatness is not necessarily the same as goodness.

—FRANK YERBY

And will you stand for what is right no matter what the cost, or how hard the fight? Or are you hoping the battle simply passes by your cubicle so that you can get back to the glory of that monthly report?

—UNKNOWN

Never think you need to apologize for asking someone to give to a worthy cause, anymore than as though you were giving him or her an opportunity to participate in a high-grade investment. The duty of giving is as much his or hers as is the duty of asking.

—JOHN D. ROCKEFELLER

A   V O L U N T E E R

Amazing how we can light tomorrow with today.

—ELIZABETH BARRETT BROWNING

In 1901 Emma Kunkle Divine, a 17-year-old Salvation Army volunteer, discovered that the busy people in the streets of New York were painfully slow in responding to the needy. What could one teenage girl do to reach so many? Emma bought a small bell and started ringing it to attract donors. The donations rolled in and soon the entire Salvation Army was ringing little bells across the nation.

Do you have a cause? If so, find your bell and ring it. Let no one tell you that the problems of the world are too big to tackle, or that one person like you can't make a difference.

—DAN ZADRA

It's amazing what ordinary people can do if they
set out without preconceived notions.

—CHARLES F. KETTERING

Just 200 years ago the average American died
by age 35. Together we've conquered smallpox,
polio and cholera—and we will soon conquer cancer.
Today, we give new hearts, lungs and eyes to our
loved ones. What you will do with your longer,
healthier life is a decision only you can make.

—DON WARD

I have been given this day to use as I will.
I can waste it or use it for good. What I do today
is important because I'm exchanging a day of
my life for it.

—UNKNOWN

T   H   E   H   E   A   R   T   O   F

Let nothing dim the light that shines from within.

—MAYA ANGELOU

At age 76, Betty Kieler organized a senior citizens
chapter of Random Acts of Kindness, and it soon
grew into one of the top volunteer organizations in her
community. By age 80, despite two major surgeries,
Betty was twice chosen one of the top ten citizens in
her community and honored as a Champion For Kids.
Even from her wheelchair she insisted, "As long as the
mouth and brain are still working, I will be there
to volunteer."

—DAN ZADRA

There is in each of us so much goodness that
if we could see its glow, it would light the world.

—SAM FRIEND

A   V   O   L   U   N   T   E   E   R

I have seen so many good deeds—people helped, lives improved—because someone cared. Do what you can to show you care about other people, and you will make our world a better place.

—ROSALYNN CARTER

Despite our success, we are not a selfish people. On the frontier, people got together to raise a neighbor's barn. Today, our friends and neighbors raise something just as important—more than $200 billion per year in charitable donations and volunteer services.

—DON WARD

The everyday kindness of the back roads more than makes up for the agony of the headlines.

—CHARLES KURALT

THE HEART OF

If the world is to be healed through human efforts,
I am convinced it will be by ordinary people—people
whose love for life is greater than their fear.

—JOANNA MACY

They called him the "Philadelphia Street Boy."
Each night Trevor Ferrell, age 12, braved the slums of
the city, providing food, blankets and clothing to street
people. Each year, in their own way, thousands of teens
pitch in to befriend the poor, sick and homeless in their
communities—but it seldom makes the news.

—DAN ZADRA

Believe that there's light at the end of the tunnel.
Believe that you might be that light for someone else.

—KOBI YAMADA

A   V   O   L   U   N   T   E   E   R

You really can change the world if you care enough.

—MARIAN WRIGHT EDELMAN

In a nation of millions and a world of billions,
the individual is still the first and basic agent
of change.

—LYNDON B. JOHNSON

Most people are like you and me, or the people
across the street or around the world from you and
me. Just like you and me, their hearts tell them that
somewhere, somehow they can make a positive
difference in the world.

—WILLIAM BAKER

The start to a better world is our belief
that it is possible.

—KATHERINE SHAW

Our arms are long enough to reach
for the tomorrow we hope for.

—LUCINDA JEFFERSON

The capacity for hope is the most significant fact of life.
It provides human beings with a sense of destination and
the energy to get started.

—NORMAN COUSINS

The first hope in our inventory—the hope that includes
and at the same time transcends all others—must be the
hope that love is going to have the last word.

—ARNOLD J. TOYNBEE

T   H   E   H   E   A   R   T   O   F

We must not only give what we have,
we must also give what we know.
—ROBERT MANN

Nearly every problem our world faces is currently being
solved in some community by some group or some
individual. Imagine if we could only get all these hearts
and minds connected so that we could collectively tackle
our problems.
—DIANE BRANSON

Never before has man had such capacity to end thirst
and hunger, to conquer poverty and disease, to banish
illiteracy. We have the power to make this the best
generation of mankind in the history of the world—
or to make it the last.
— JOHN F. KENNEDY

A   V   O   L   U   N   T   E   E   R

We have to find ways of organizing ourselves with the rest of humanity. It has to be everybody or nobody.

—BUCKMINSTER FULLER

What was most significant about the lunar voyage was not that men set foot on the moon but that they set eye on the earth.

—NORMAN COUSINS

To see the earth as we now see it, small and beautiful in that eternal silence where it floats, is to see ourselves as riders on the earth together, brothers on that bright loveliness in the unending light.

—ARCHIBALD MACLEISH

Think globally, but act locally.
—RENE DUBOS

Responsibility does not only lie with the leaders
of our countries or communities or with those who have
been appointed or elected to do a particular job. It lies
with each of us individually.
—THE DALAI LAMA

Somewhere on this planet, someone has a solution to
each of the world's problems. It might be one of us.
With your help, we can build a more hopeful world.
—MARIANNE LARNED

A   V   O   L   U   N   T   E   E   R

How do you want to be remembered?

—KOBI YAMADA

You will find, as you look back upon your life, that the moments when you really lived are the moments when you have done things in the spirit of love.

—HENRY DRUMMOND

What the heart gives away is never gone.
It is kept in the hearts of others.

—ROBIN ST. JOHN

Strange, isn't it George, how each man's life touches so many others, and when he isn't around it leaves an awful hole?

—CLARENCE THE ANGEL, "IT'S A WONDERFUL LIFE"

The measure of life is not its duration but its donation.

When you cease to make a contribution, you begin to die.

When you stop giving and offering something to the rest of the world, it's time to turn out the lights.

T   H   E   H   E   A   R   T   O   F

What if the rest of your life was the best
of your life?

—KOBI YAMADA

Don't waste too much of the time you have left.
Make some piece of the world care.

—ROBERT B. HORTON

You are being interviewed on your 100th birthday.
What would you really like to be able to tell that
reporter about your life? Now flip back to today
and start fresh.

—KEYNOTE

A   V   O   L   U   N   T   E   E   R

Here is the test to find whether or not your mission on earth is finished: If you are alive, it isn't.

—RICHARD BACH

May this be the year that we take the time to be friends who don't need to be asked, who teach, who keep dreams alive, who only lift.

—DALE DAUTEN

May happiness touch your life today as warmly as you have touched the lives of others.

—REBECCA FORSYTHE

The good you do is not lost though you forget it.
—JIRI MASALA

We leave you a tradition for the future: The tender loving care of human beings must never become obsolete. People even more than things, have to be restored, renewed, revived, reclaimed, redeemed and redeemed and redeemed. Never throw anyone away.
—UNKNOWN

Your heart has brought great joy to many.
Those hearts can never forget you.
—FLAVIA WEEDEN

A V O L U N T E E R